639

JAN 2 9 2002

Go
To
Sleep,
Baby
Child

Go To Sleep, Baby Child

62 Favorite Lullabies to Soothe Your Baby

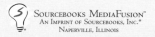

SOURCEBOOKS MEDIAFUSION™
AN IMPRINT OF SOURCEBOOKS, INC.®
NAPERVILLE, ILLINOIS

Published by Sourcebooks, Inc.
P.O. Box 4410, Naperville, Illinois 60567-4410
(630) 961-3900
FAX: (630) 961-2168
www.sourcebooks.com

ISBN 1-57071-835-0

Printed and bound in China
IM   10 9 8 7 6 5 4 3 2 1

This book is dedicated to sleeping babies everywhere.

Table of Contents

SONG	PAGE/CD TRACK

Baby's Name:

Birthplace:

Birthday:

Day of the Week:

Time:

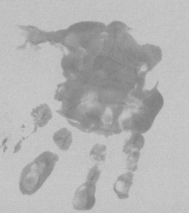

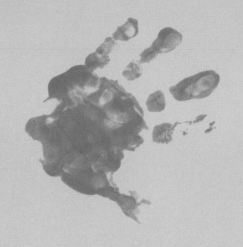

Weight:

Length:

Eye Color:

Hair Color:

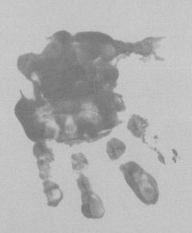

Mother:

Grandmother:

Grandfather:

Brothers:

Father:

Grandmother:

Grandfather:

Sisters:

sleeping baby
photo here

date

_____

favorite song
to fall asleep to

_____

Introduction

What sound is more angelic than a mother's voice lulling her baby to sleep with song? What musical instrument can compare to the sonorous timbre of a father's hushed tones when soothing his child to slumber? And is there any nostalgia more poignantly felt than that which washes over us as we gaze lovingly at our own babies, finally sleeping after a busy day and perhaps a fussy bedtime? Tired as a parent may be after walking and rocking, singing and hoping, it can be difficult to tear yourself away from that warm, sweet, sleeping little one. With the melodies of lullabies playing gently through your head—perhaps you're still even humming—you tiptoe quietly out of the nursery and tip the door half-shut behind you.

There is a magical essence to lullabies that makes them universal and timeless. These "cradle songs," named for their lulling tones, can be found in the music of any country and every culture regardless of the time period. An interesting bit of

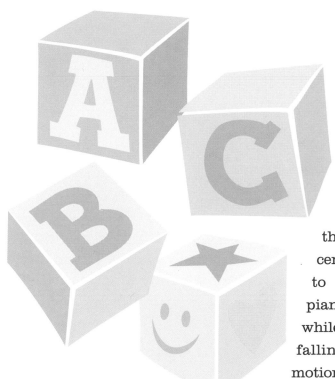

their history comes from the nineteenth century, when it was common for lullabies to be composed as piano pieces. The pianist's right hand varied the melody while the left hand sounded out rising and falling notes. The combination of the motions as the hands danced along the keys mimicked the rocking of a cradle. The practical and technical elements of the musical composition, such as the 6/8 time, were maintained, and yet the musicians were allowed a considerable range of creative freedom to conjure up enchanting and tranquil tunes.

Formal musical criteria aside, the true beauty of lullabies is the way the music embraces the words, and they move together rhythmically—not unlike a parent swaying back and forth, gently rubbing baby's back—in an intimate expression of love and comfort. The incomparable bond that exists between parent and child is recreated in the melding of lyrics and melodies.

Bedtime routines are special times of closeness; lullabies quickly and naturally fit themselves into the pattern. But more than just pleasant niceties, the songs can be beneficial sleep aids as well. Recently, it has been shown that children who are sung to early and often begin to speak and read earlier than others. Even before infants' sense of hearing is perfected, they prefer the human voice to almost any other sound. Because they provide ample opportunity for a baby to connect with voices singing, lullabies take on an important role in the development of language skills.

Enjoy these lullabies with your baby and play them over and over to your heart's content. All children are charmed by the sound of music, and if you linger for a little while longer after your young one has drifted off, the familiar songs may have a soothing effect on your spirits as well.

Go To Sleep, Baby Child

If only they could
stay small forever!

All the Pretty Little Horses

Go to sleep baby child,
Go to sleep my little baby,
Hush-a-bye, don't you cry,
Go to sleep my little baby.
When you wake you will have
All the pretty little horses.
Blacks and grays, dapples and bays
Coach and six little horses.
Hush-a-bye, don't you cry,
Go to sleep my little baby.

Brahms' Lullaby

Lullaby and goodnight
With roses bedight
With lilies be spread
Is baby's wee bed,
Lay thee down now and rest
May thy slumber be blessed,
Lay thee down now and rest
May thy slumber be blessed.

I Love Little Pussy

I love little pussy, her coat is so warm,
And if I don't hurt her, she'll do me no harm.
I'll sit by the fire and give her some food.
And pussy will love me...because I am good.
I love little doggie, his nose is so cold.
When he sees a stranger, he acts fierce and bold.
I'll feed him and walk him without fail each day.
And doggie be will there...when I want to play.
I love my new pony, he's so neat and trim,
And we'll both enjoy it when I ride on him.
I've only one problem—a name for my pony.
I know what I'll do...I'll just call him "Tony."

Kum Ba Yah

Kum ba yah yah, Kum ba yah
Kum ba yah yah, Kum ba yah
Kum ba yah yah, Kum ba yah
Oh, Oh, Kum ba yah!

4
SONG

Mary Had a Little Lamb

Mary had a little lamb,
Little lamb, little lamb,
Mary had a little lamb,
Its fleece was white as snow.
It followed her to school one day,
School one day, school one day,
It followod hor to oohool ono day,
Which was against the rule.
It made the children laugh and play,
Laugh and play, laugh and play,
It made the children laugh and play,
To see a lamb at school.
And so the teacher turned it out,
Turned it out, turned it out,
And so the teacher turned it out,
But still it lingered near.
What makes the lamb love Mary so,
Mary so, Mary so?
What makes the lamb love Mary so?
The eager children cried.
Why Mary loves the lamb you know,
Lamb you know, lamb you know,
Why, Mary loves the lamb you know,
The teacher did reply.

Rock-a-Bye Baby

Rock-a-bye baby, on the tree top,
When the wind blows, the cradle will rock.
When the bow breaks, the cradle will fall
And down will come baby, cradle and all.

Hey Diddle Diddle

Hey diddle diddle,
The cat and the fiddle,
The cow jumped over the moon,
The little dog laughed to see such sport,
And the dish ran away with the spoon.
Hey diddle diddle,
The cat and the fiddle,
The cow jumped over the moon,
The little dog laughed to see such sport,
And the dish ran away with the spoon.

What Shall We Do?

What shall we do when we all go out,
All go out, all go out?
What shall we do when we all go out,
When we all go out to play?
We will ride our 3-wheel bikes,
3-wheel bikes, 3-wheel bikes.
We will ride our 3-wheel bikes
When we all go out to play.
We will skate on roller skates,
Roller skates, roller skates.
We will skate on roller skates
When we all go out to play.
We will see saw up and down,
Up and down, up and down.
We will see saw up and down
When we all go out to play.
What shall we do when we all go out,
All go out, all go out?
What shall we do when we all go out,
When we all go out to play?

Pat-a-Cake

Pat-a-cake, Pat-a-cake, baker's man,
Bake me a cake just as fast as you can.
Pat it, and shape it, and mark it with "B,"
And put it in the oven for baby and me.
Pat-a-cake, Pat-a-cake, baker's man,
Bake me a cake just as fast as you can.
Pat it, and shape it, and mark it with "B,"
And put it in the oven for baby and me.

Nocturne (by Borodin)

Here in twilight's soft glow
Time to go to bed to slumber.
Our darling child these sweet dreams be yours
To fill your sleeping hours.
Now evening shadows fall.
Sleepy time is calling.
Close your eyes,
Warm in sleep,
Safe in your parents' love.
Our love is yours forever,
Our love is yours forever.

Bedtime Song

Tell me a tale of kings and queens,
Tell me of Peter Pan.
Tell me of when you were a boy,
Of when I shall be a man.
I like to sit here in the dark,
Listening to all you say.
I feel so lonesome in my bed,
I wish you would let me stay.

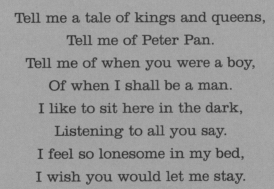

Wind in the Willow

Lie down baby on your pillow,
The wind is whisperin' in the willow.
Lie down baby do not weep,
Lie down and sleep.
Lie down baby on your pillow,
The wind is whisperin' in the willow.
Lie down baby do not weep,
Lie down and sleep.

Morning (by Grieg)

Each day at dawning,
My baby is yawning,
Not ready to start a new day.
Then baby starts smiling,
With ways so beguiling
When she thinks it's now time for play.
I love your nose,
And your feet and your toes,
I love your bright little eyes.
I love your giggle,
And I love your wiggle,
I love your dear little sighs.
When you will leave me, I know it will grieve me,
I know how the years will fly by.

(13)
SONG

Baby Bye, Here's a Fly

Baby bye, here's a fly,
We will watch him, you and I,
How he crawls, up the walls
Yet he never falls.

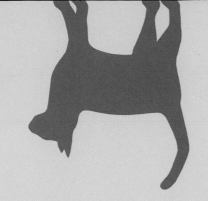

Three Little Kittens

Once three little kittens, they lost their mittens

And they began to cry.

Oh mother dear, we sadly fear

Our mittens we have lost.

What, lost your mittens? You naughty kittens!

Then you shall have no pie.

Meow, meow, meow, meow.

The three little kittens, they found their mittens

And they began to cry.

Oh mother dear, see here, see here!

Our mittens we have found.

What, found your mittens, you darling kittens,

Then you shall have some pie.

Meow, meow, meow, meow.

Twinkle, Twinkle Little Star

Twinkle, twinkle little star
How I wonder what you are,
Up above the world so high
Like a diamond in the sky,
Twinkle, twinkle little star
How I wonder what you are.
In the dark blue sky you keep
Often through my curtains peep,
For you never shut your eye
'Til the sun is in the sky,
Twinkle, twinkle little star
How I wonder what you are.

Peas Porridge Hot

Peas Porridge hot,

Peas Porridge cold,

Peas Porridge in the pot nine days old.

Some like it hot,

Some like it cold,

Some like it in the pot nine days old.

Peas Porridge hot,

Peas Porridge cold,

Peas Porridge in the pot nine days old.

Pussy Cat, Pussy Cat

Pussy cat, Pussy cat, where have you been?
I've been to London to visit the Queen.
Pussy cat, Pussy cat, what did you there?
I frightened a little mouse under her chair.
Pussy cat, Pussy cat, where have you been?
I've been to New York, oh what a scene.
Pussy cat, Pussy cat, what did you there?
Looked at the buildings that soared in the air.

Two Birds on a Stone

There were two birds
Sat on a stone,
Fa la la la la de.
One flew away and
Then there was one,
Fa la la la la de.
The other flew after and
Then there was none,
Fa la la la la de.
And so the poor stone
Was left all alone.
Fa la la la la de.

Golden Slumbers

Golden slumbers kiss your eyes,
Smiles awake you when you rise;
Sleep pretty loved ones, do not cry,
And I will sing a lullaby,
Lullaby, lullaby, lullaby.

Jack and Jill

Jack and Jill went up the hill
To fetch a pail of water.
Jack fell down and broke his crown,
And Jill came tumbling after.
Up Jack got and home did trot,
As fast as he could caper.
Went to bed to mend his head,
With vinegar and brown paper.
Jill came in and she did grin,
To see his paper plaster.
Mother vexed,
Did scold her next,
For laughing at Jack's disaster.

Little Drops of Water

Little drops of water,
Little grains of sand,
Make the mighty ocean
And the pleasant land.
Little ships must keep the shore,
Larger ships may venture more.
Little drops of water,
Little grains of sand,
Make the mighty ocean
And the pleasant land.

Dinosaurs in Dreamland

Go to sleep, little one,
In my arms here tonight.
While you sleep, little one,
Everything will be all right.
Dinosaurs in Dreamland
Will keep you in sight
Standing close while you sleep
Through the night.
So go to sleep, little one,
There's so much you can share.
As you sleep, little one,
Make a wish and you'll be there.
Dinosaurs in Dreamland
Are keeping you in sight
Standing close while you sleep tonight.

Sleep Now and Rest
(from Russia)

Sleep my baby, sleep now and rest,
Safe as a fledgling in its sweet nest.
Sleep now and rest, safe in your nest,
Sleep my baby sleep.

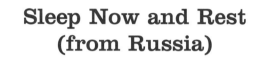

24
SONG

Nature's Goodnight

Clouds of gray are in the sky,
Flocks of birds are winging by,
Trees now dressed in faded brown,
Send their leaves all rustling down.
Little flowers in slumber deep,
Nod their drowsy heads and sleep.
All the world must say "Good Night,"
'Til spring comes back with sunshine bright.

Barcarolle (by Offenbach)

In my arms
My little one rests,
I hold her so safe and snug.
Baby dear,
Your parents are here,
We kiss and we hold and hug.
Now go to sleep,
Just close your eyes
And dream the night away.
Starlight bright,
Moon's glowing light
Until the break of day.
Breezes brush your cheek
In morning's sweet embrace.
Open up your eyes
With a smile on your face.
Now in my arms
My little one rests.

Greensleeves

Alas, my love, you do me wrong,
To cast me out discourteously
When I have loved you so long,
Delighting in your company.
Greensleeves was my delight,
Greensleeves was my heart of gold,
Greensleeves was my lady love,
And who but my lady Greensleeves.
I have been ready at your hand
To grant whatever you would crave.
I have both wagered life and land,
Your love and good will for to have.

Where Are You Going to, My Pretty Maid?

Where are you going to, my pretty maid?
I'm going a-milking sir, she said,
Sir, she said, sir, she said,
I'm going a-milking sir, she said.
May I go with you, my pretty maid?
You're kindly welcome, sir, she said,
Sir, she said, sir, she said.
You're kindly welcome, sir, she said.

Stars in the Sky
(from Poland)

Lullaby, the stars are in the sky
The moon is up on high
Lullaby.
Sleep, lullaby,
Sleep, lullaby,
Sleep, lullaby,
Lullaby.

**㉙
SONG**

The Baby and the Moon

Lady Moon, Lady Moon, sailing on high,
Come down to baby from out of the sky.
Baby dear, baby dear, down far below,
I hear you calling, I hear you calling,
I hear you calling, yet I cannot go.

Once I Saw a Little Bird

Once I saw a little bird come hop, hop, hop.

And I cried little bird will you stop, stop, stop?

I was going to the window to say how do you do?

But he shook his little tail and away he flew.

Once I saw a little bird come hop, hop, hop.

And I cried little bird will you stop, stop, stop?

Humpty Dumpty

Humpty Dumpty sat on a wall,
Humpty Dumpty had a great fall.
All the king's horses,
And all the king's men,
Couldn't put Humpty together again.
Humpty Dumpty sat on a wall,
Humpty Dumpty had a great fall.
All the king's horses,
And all the king's men,
Couldn't put Humpty together again.

Three White Gulls

There are three white gulls a-flying,
There are three white gulls a-flying,
There are three white gulls a-flying.
  By the sea they cry,
  By the sea they cry,
  By the sea they cry.
  By the sea they cry,
  By the sea they cry,
  By the sea they cry.

33
SONG

Winkum, Winkum

Winkum, Winkum, shut your eyes.
Sweet my baby, lullaby,
For the dews are falling soft,
Lights are flickering up aloft,
And the moon lights peeping over
Yonder hilltop, capped with clover.
Chickens long have gone to rest,
Birds lie snug within their nest.
And my birdie soon will be
Sleeping like a chick-a-dee.
For with only half a try,
Winkum, Winkum shuts her eye.
For with only half a try,
Winkum, Winkum shuts her eye.

Little Bo Peep

Little Bo Peep has lost her sheep
And can't tell where to find them.
Leave them alone and they'll come home,
Wagging their tails behind them.

Now the Day Is Over

Now the day is over,
Night is drawing nigh.
Shadows of the evening
Steal across the sky.

Gently Sleep
(from Hungary)

Little baby gently sleep,
Do not weep.
I will keep you safe and warm,
I will keep you, keep you, keep you,
I will keep you safe and warm.
Little baby gently sleep,
I will keep you safe from harm.

Sleep, Baby Sleep

Sleep, baby sleep.
Your father tends the sheep,
Your mother shakes the dreamland tree,
Down falls a little dream for thee.
Sleep, baby sleep.
Sleep, baby sleep.
Sleep, baby sleep.

All Through the Night

Sleep, my child, and peace attend thee,
All through the night.
Guardian angels God will send thee,
All though the night.
Soft the drowsy hours are creeping,
Hill and vale in slumber steeping,
I my loving vigil keeping,
All though the night.

Ode to Joy (by Beethoven)

Stars in heaven high above us,
In your bright and sparkling glow.
On my babe's face cast your magic,
Light his path where e'er he go.
Strong and tender,
Warm, kind, and caring,
He shall grow to manhood proud.
May his days be filled with splendor,
May his head remain unbowed.

Little Boy Blue

Little boy blue, come blow your horn,
The sheep's in the meadow, the cow's in the corn.
Where is the boy who looks after the sheep?
He's under the haystack, fast asleep.
He's under the haystack, fast asleep.

Mozart's Lullaby

Sleep, little one, go to sleep,
Mother is here by thy bed.
Sleep, little one, go to sleep,
Rest on thy pillow thy head.
The world is silent and still,
The moon shines bright on the hill,
And creeps past thy windowsill.
Sleep, little one, go to sleep.
Oh sleep, go to sleep.

Ride a Cock Horse

Ride a cock horse to Banbury Cross,
To see a fine lady upon a white horse.
Rings on her fingers and bells on her toes,
She shall have music wherever she goes.

Bluebird, Bluebird

Bluebird, bluebird through my window.
Bluebird, bluebird through my window.
Bluebird, bluebird through my window.
Oh, Johnny aren't you tired?
Find a little friend and tap him on the shoulder.
Find a little friend and tap him on the shoulder.
Find a little friend and tap him on the shoulder.
Oh, Johnny aren't you tired?
Catch a shooting star and put it in your pocket.
Catch a shooting star and put it in your pocket.
Catch a shooting star and put it in your pocket.
Oh, Johnny aren't you tired?
Oh, Johnny aren't you tired?

Can You Count the Stars?

Can you count the stars
Twinkling brightly in the midnight sky?
Can you count the clouds
Lightly o'er the meadows floating by?
You and I can count their number
With our eyes so close to slumber,
Shining always every one.

Sweet Be Your Sleep

Goodnight to you all and sweet be your sleep.
May angels around you their silent watch keep.
Goodnight, Goodnight, Goodnight, Goodnight.
Goodnight to you all and sweet be your sleep.
May angels around you their silent watch keep.
May angels around you their silent watch keep.
Goodnight, Goodnight, Goodnight, Goodnight.
Goodnight, Goodnight, Goodnight, Goodnight.
Goodnight, Goodnight, Goodnight, Goodnight.

Two Black Birds

There were two black birds,
Sat upon a hill.
The one was named Jack,
The other named Jill.
Fly away Jack, fly away Jill.
Come again Jack,
Come again Jill.
There were two black birds,
Sat upon a hill.
The one was named Jack,
The other named Jill.
Fly away Jack, fly away Jill.
Come again Jack,
Come again Jill.

Cantata 147
(by Bach)

Time to sleep,
To dream of fairies.
Close your eyes now,
Sleepyhead.
Just one more hug,
So safe and snug.

Comin' Through the Rye

If a lassie meet her laddie comin' through the rye,
If a lassie kiss a laddie, need a laddie cry?
Every lassie has her laddie, none they say have I yet,
All the lads, they smile on me when comin' through the rye.
If a body meet a body comin' through the rye,
If a body kiss a body, need a body cry?
Every lassie has her laddie, none they say have I yet,
All the lads they smile on me when comin' through the rye.

Sleep My Child

Sleep my child, my princeling rest,
Go to sleep, slumber deep, sleep my child on mother's breast.
Mother's here, never fear.
Sleep my child. My princeling go to sleep.
The world is waiting while you sleep,
And heaven's angels watch will keep.
The world is waiting while you sleep,
And heaven's angels watch will keep.

50
SONG

Sing a Song of Sixpence

Sing a song of sixpence,
A pocket full of rye;
Four and twenty blackbirds
Baked in a pie!
When the pie was opened,
The birds began to sing;
Wasn't that a dainty dish
To set before the king?
The king was in his counting house,
Counting out his money;
The queen was in the parlor,
Eating bread and honey.
The maid was in the garden,
Hanging out the clothes;
Along came a blackbird
And nipped off her nose!
Sing a song of sixpence,
A pocket full of rye;
Four and twenty blackbirds
Baked in a pie!
When the pie was opened,
The birds began to sing;
Wasn't that a dainty dish
To set before the king?

Little Robin Redbreast

Little Robin Redbreast sat upon a tree,
Up went pussy cat and down flew he.
Down came pussy cat, away Robin ran,
Said little Robin Redbreast, catch me if you can.
Little Robin Redbreast jumped upon a wall,
Pussy cat jumped after him and almost had a fall.
Little Robin chirped and sang and what did pussy say,
Pussy cat said "meow" and Robin flew away.

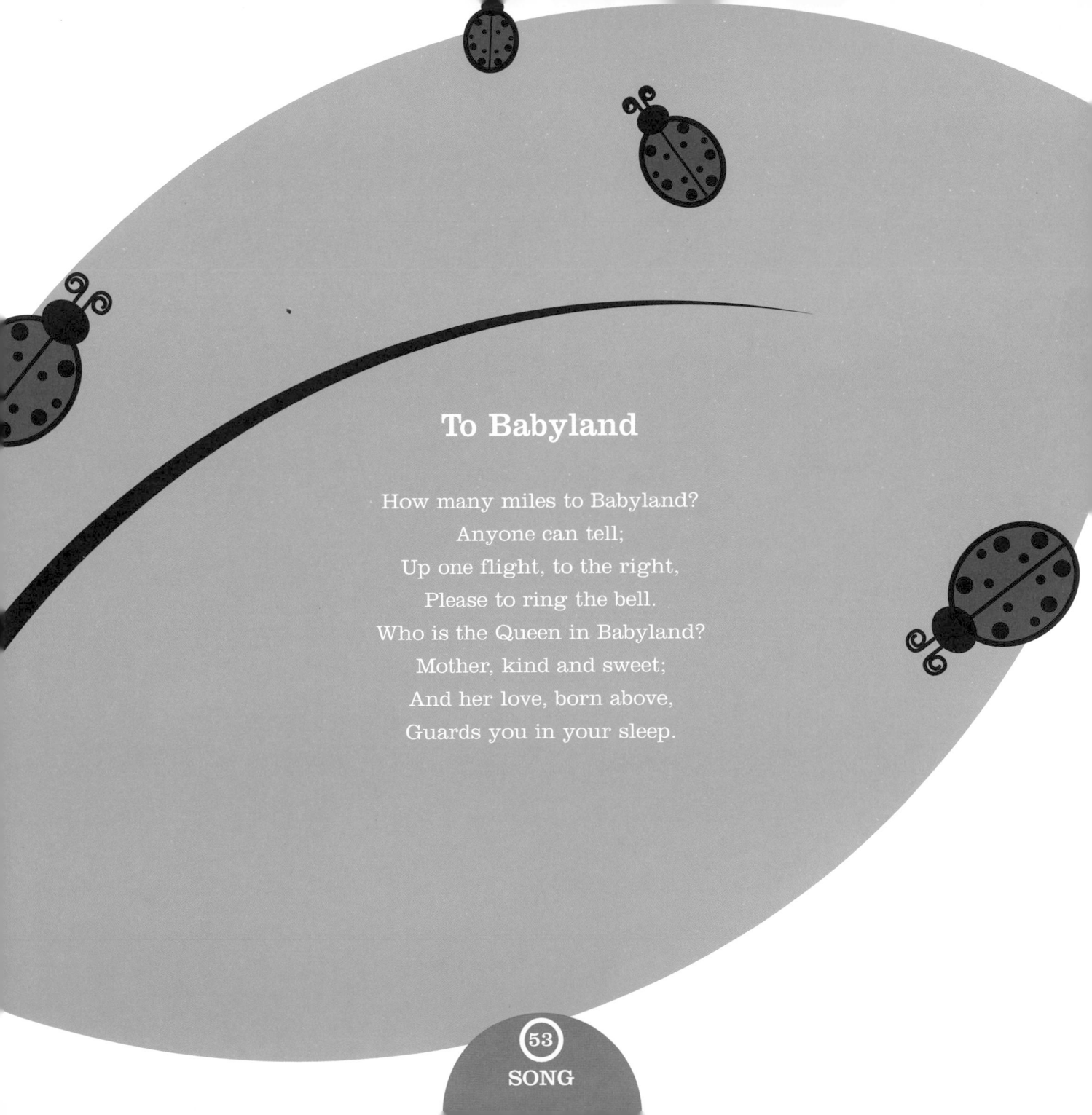

To Babyland

How many miles to Babyland?
Anyone can tell;
Up one flight, to the right,
Please to ring the bell.
Who is the Queen in Babyland?
Mother, kind and sweet;
And her love, born above,
Guards you in your sleep.

The Sandman Will Come

Sleep, sleep, my little baby,
Don't cry anymore.
Soon the Sandman will come
To take you away to Dreamland.
Soon the Sandman will come
To take you away to Dreamland.
Soon the Sandman will come
To take you away to Dreamland.

Oh How Lovely Is the Evening

Oh how lovely is the evening, is the evening
When the bells are sweetly ringing, sweetly ringing.
Oh how lovely is the evening, is the evening
When the bells are sweetly ringing, sweetly ringing,
Ding dong, ding dong, ding dong.

A B C Song

A, B, C, D, E, F, G,
H, I, J, K, L, M, N, O, P,
Q, R, S, T, U, V,
W, X, Y, and Z.
Now you know your ABCs,
This time will you sing with me?

Down by the River

Down by the river where the green grass grows,
There sits Sally washing her clothes,
She sings, she sings, she sings so sweet,
And she calls her playmates up and down the street.
Mary, Mary, won't you come to tea?
Come next Saturday at half past three,
Tea cakes and pancakes and everything you see,
Oh won't we have a jolly time at half past three?
Down by the river where the flowers all smile,
There sits Sally laughing all the while,
She sings, she sings, she sings so sweet,
And she calls her playmates up and down the street.
Janie, Janie, won't you come to tea?
Come next Saturday at half past three,
Cookies and pastries and everything you see,
Oh won't we have a jolly time at half past three?
Oh won't we have a jolly time at half past three?

Down in the Valley

Down in the valley,
Valley so low,
Hang your head over,
Hear the wind blow.
Hear the wind blow dear,
Hear the wind blow.
Hang your head over,
Hear the wind blow.

Sleepy Time

Sleepy time has come for my baby,

Baby now is going to sleep.

Kiss mama good night,

And we'll turn out the light,

While I tuck you in bed,

'Neath your covers tight.

Sleepy time has come for my baby,

Baby now is going to sleep.

Goodnight.

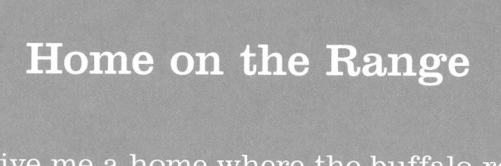

Home on the Range

Oh give me a home where the buffalo roam,
Where the deer and the antelope play.
Where seldom is heard a discouraging word,
And the skies are not cloudy all day.
Home, home on the range,
Where the deer and the antelope play.
Where seldom is heard a discouraging word,
And the skies are not cloudy all day.

Lavender's Blue

Lavender's blue, dilly, dilly,
Lavender's green,
When you are king, dilly, dilly,
I shall be queen.
Who told you so, dilly, dilly,
Who told you so?
'Twas my own heart, dilly, dilly,
That told me so.

Hush Little Baby

Hush little baby, don't say a word,
Papa's gonna buy you a mockingbird.
If that mockingbird don't sing,
Papa's gonna buy you a diamond ring.
If that diamond ring turns brass,
Papa's gonna buy you a looking glass.
If that looking glass gets broke,
Papa's gonna buy you a billy goat.
Hush little baby, don't you cry,
Mama's gonna sing you a lullaby.
Hush little baby,
Hush little baby,
Hush.